Maddie the Mathematician
The Adventure Begins

http://maddiethemathematician.com/
https://www.facebook.com/maddielovesmath/
http://about.me/nneniajoseph
nnenia.joseph@gmail.com

Copyright © 2015 Nnenia Joseph, Ph. D
Illustrations ©2015 Al Danso
ISBN: 978-1-936937-88-2

All Rights Reserved. No part of this book may be reproduced, stored in retrieval systems, or transmitted in any form, by any means, including mechanical, electronic, photocopying recording, or otherwise without prior written permission of the author and publisher.

Printed in The United States of America.

Dedication

I would like to dedicate this book to my daughter Xenovia. I want her to know that mathematics is all around us and it has the potential to open many doors. Learning the language of math is the key to success. Remember not to let the challenges of mathematics prevent you from trying. I want you to continue to do your best and always think before you do.

Maddie was a very curious girl, who always thought numbers were special. She would find numbers everywhere she went. Maddie would discover numbers in her room, as she counted her fluffy animals. She also noticed numbers in the kitchen, when she counted eggs to help her mother cook.

Even on the way to school Maddie would find numbers. She counted the people, buildings and cars. Maddie would find numbers everywhere!

One day her teacher Ms. Burkett, told her that numbers were a part of the amazing system of mathematics. Maddie's eyes grew big with curiosity. She just had to find out more about math!

That day in class Maddie looked for numbers all day. She saw sets of numbers, digits and symbols that represented numbers. Maddie noticed the class pest, Samuel, playing with a set of blocks. She noticed how he arranged the blocks in various sets. Maddie put on her observation eyes and noticed that Samuel was creating a pattern.

He placed one red block, 2 green blocks, 3 blue blocks, 4 red blocks, 5 green blocks and 6 blue. If the pattern continued Maddie knew she could figure out what the next set would be.

She stood there thinking about the pattern. She soon knew that the next set Samuel would represent would be 7 red blocks. As Maddie watched Samuel place red blocks on the carpet and continue his pattern Maddie became excited!

At recess, Maddie was really excited about her discovery, so she decided to observe some more math. She noticed there were 6 swings and 2 slides on the playground. She also saw there were 2 seesaws and 1 jungle gym. The playground was full of numbers!

At the end of the day, Maddie thought about all her observations. She saw numbers everywhere! Did this mean math was everywhere? When Maddie got home she knew what she wanted to be. It was her goal to become a mathematician. From that day forward she introduced herself as Maddie the Mathematician!

Hi, I'm Maddie, and math is my thing! If you like math, let me hear you sing. One-Two-Three, math is for me; Four-Five-Six, math's a quick fix; Seven-Eight-Nine, we do it every time! Next comes 10 and we can solve it again.

Now let's begin our math adventure!

About the Author

Nnenia Joseph (Hill) has been an educator for 12 years. She has first-hand knowledge of the difficulties children have with mathematics. In an effort to help her own daughter she created Maddie the Mathematician. She hopes Maddie helps children have fun with math and understand that mathematics is all around.

"Lifelong learning is the key to success and overall social development"- Nnenia Joseph

Maddiethemathematician.com

https://www.facebook.com/maddielovesmath/

www.ingramcontent.com/pod-product-compliance
Lightning Source LLC
Chambersburg PA
CBHW042314280426
43661CB00101B/1256